A Storm in Arcadia

A Storm in Arcadia

poems

Ron Carey

Clare Songbirds
Publishing House

Clare Songbirds Publishing House Poetry Series
ISBN 978-1-957221-27-4
Clare Songbirds Publishing House
A Storm in Arcadia © 2025 Ron Carey

Printed in the United States of America
FIRST EDITION

Cover painting *The Storm* by Pierre-Auguste Cot 1880 courtesy
of the Metropolitan Museum of Art open access

140 Cottage Street
Auburn, New York 13021
www.claresongbirdspub.com

To my Mum and Dad, Lily and Bill Carey. Their love and kindness still touches and inspires me.

Some of the poems in this collection have featured in other publications.

László Kovács and His Sons Cross the Border.- The Gregory O' Donoghue International Poetry Prize, Southward Magazine and the Irish Times.

Morning : Rathfarnham - The Irish Times

The Burning of the Books, On Writing a Poem on the Love Life of Walt Whitman Outside the Changing Rooms at Marks and Spencer and Inchydoney - Elizabeth Royal Patton Poetry Prize Anthology.

Shooting Michael Collins, The Trade – Live Encounters, Online Magazine 2022.

Contents

A Storm in Arcadia

Once I had a dream that we were lost in Arcadia,
A storm coming.
Not a real storm – there are no real storms in Arcadia.
And the darkness was wonderful as on
A crackled canvas, with imaginative lightning
And booms of thunder arriving late.
Shepherds, their faces beautiful with the beauty
Of mortal men, brought their frightened sheep
Down to the safety of the valley.
The rain that fell was young and kind, suffused
With salt from Thessalonica's gilded coast.
Inside a shelter, heavy with love, we listened
As the old man told his story.
How, one night, he met the Wolf King, Lycaon,
Who roared at the sky until the stars trembled
And fell into the sea.
Then the storm faded and I woke, blessed
To have you beside me.
Outside, real birds began to sing, filling
The garden with songs a hundred million years old.

Adam's Grave

There was no one to show him how to die.
So he waited.
Waited until time had eaten away his perfect body.
He did not despair.
But could give no reason for his acceptance.
Perhaps failure was a seed in the mud
From which he was created.
And then, the light of Heaven went out
Of his beautiful, sky-blue eyes, the way
It fades from the eyes of babies the moment
After they are born.
Then he closed, like a flower.
They returned him to the earth,
Filling his grave with blood-red apples.

On Writing a Poem on the Love Life of Walt Whitman Outside the Changing Rooms at Marks and Spencer

The black bears roll between summer skirts and sandals.
The deer are rutting in a forest of jeans, manifestly horned.
The women, natural, good-humoured, patient, flagged
In multi-coloured choices—ignore, at the changing door,
The candour of my waiting.
Far off, under the sparkling eyes of war, I hear the boys
In blue and grey go marching, down the third floor,
Air-conditioned, corridors of splendour.
The Wound Dresser bends to kiss the forehead of a dying soldier
And all that is human in me fills with tenderness.

I keep writing but I am distracted by the affable assistant.
Her bubbly personality retails confidence to young and old alike.
Her mind rejects all that is negative.
My wife emerges empty handed and unsatisfied.
As we ride the escalator down to Parking, its rattle reminds me
Of that winter night when Walt found love on a Washington tram.
We drive out into the sunlight of a Dublin suburb.
Beyond the settled houses, buffalo cover the plains in shadow.

If You Know How a Boreen Sometimes

If you know how a boreen sometimes tunnels the light,
You will know how it came delving towards me, carrying
The black outline of a man.
His face wore the generations of a settled people.
His eyes green with land.
His persona as sharp and awkward as hawthorn.
He asked me what in God's name brought me
Here, to this out-of-the-way place, as if his owning it
Was a separate thing—already my going was in his voice.
I answered it was poetry, poetry brought me.
He turned and looked at the fields—the way
A shepherd might remember a lost sheep.
Finally, he nodded, satisfied with whatever bargain
He made with himself.
Then, with nothing agreed, we walked on together, while
The wet day shook itself vigorously in the sun.

The Death of Peter Pan

Peter Llewelyn Davies was identified as the original Peter Pan and it plagued him all his life. He committed suicide at London's Slone Square Underground Station in 1960.

In the Underground, between the clash
And quarrels of steel, while he waits, his train
To Kensington has come and gone.
Now that the affection of the Royal Court Bar
Has faded, the pungent smell
Of tropical vegetation fills his head –
The old hook of another migraine.
From the darkness of the tunnel comes
The laughter of wicked boys, bringing
Memories that pass as quickly as his smile.
Suddenly, unnoticed by the adults,
His shadow breaks away, leaping light
As a fairy on the green-tiled walls.
Now it races down the crowded platform
And into the Pirate Cave.
What else can a lost boy do, but follow?

Inchydoney

Here, on the light-skinned beach at Inchydoney, with the tide
So far out it looks like it might never return, even
If you don't believe in God you must admit
Someone is really good on the details.
Take that cormorant sweeping the waves, head
Tilted towards a sky of mirrors, with all its skim
And swiftness lowered, almost cresting, almost touching.
And now another, following the same path, a path invisible
To the eye, spun in colour and the power of flight.
And down they come, holding their wings out to dry
In September's fast fading.
I think they must be a pair, see how they bend their question
Shaped heads, too close to be anything but lovers.
Though your hand has been in mine all day, I suddenly feel it,
Warm and wonderfully alive, like a small bird in its nest.

Note on Richard Feynman's Physics Lecture –
Photons, Corpuscles of Light

It was the word that stopped me moving on.
Corpuscles—a word lovely of itself, needing
To be nothing but itself, locked in its own sound.
This led me to the idea of red and white blood cells
Infused with light, pulsating through the universe
Of the body before its final Resurrection.
Which is a mad idea.
But no crazier then Feynman explaining
How Nature works on probability.
That it won't conform and cannot be pinned down.
And this resonated with me, perhaps because this is how
I try to live my own improbable life.
I worked to stay with him as he tunnelled below the sub-atomic,
Where scientists use quantum-mechanics to hunt for God.
He had a lovely smile and he smiled at the thought
That light photons, reflecting the Moon in the water,
Were subject to chance—without ever once telling us
If the water was an ocean or a pond or if the Moon was full.

The Cloud of Kalidasa at Lough Derg

Kalidasa (4th–5th century CE) was a Classical Sanskrit author who is often considered ancient India's greatest poet. The Cloud Messenger is one of his best known poems.

Today, my soul is almost outside my body.
So close to the surface it feels the heat of the sun.
I should drive on but I'm held.
As if I knew I would see something wonderful.
And there it is.
A white-tailed eagle flying above the summer waters
Of Lough Derg to the old, ruined church at Inis Cealtra.
        Time.
The sun is still in its high benediction as I watch
A lone cloud drifts over the lake.
Once, it would have brought to mind Wordsworth's introspection,
But today it is Kalidasa's joyful traveller that takes
The heavenly path, as once it soared
Over trees, flowers, cities and the temple-towns.
Where the rivers wave to the cloud, their hero.
Where the mountains call it to rest among friends.
        Time.
Now, the dark is stirring and I turn for home.
Night rushes towards me and lights up the car with a kiss.

Maria Rasputin Pulls Double-Shift in Miami Docks

Maria Rasputin was the daughter of Grigori Rasputin. She was a dancer in a show about the life and death of her father, a lion tamer and a riveter in the USA during the 2nd World War. She died in Los Angeles in 1977.

Gideon Walrave Boissevain loves her.
It's the one true thing she knows for sure.
And he thinks she's hot—hot as the molten shipyard
Rivets she slings across the war, while Americans
And Russians save the world, one more time.
It doesn't pay as much as having your own circus act
Or being in a show, the bees-knees in sarafan and tiara,
While dancing to the tragedy of your father's death.
And there is nothing mystical in the faces
Of New York actors with their fake, unholy darkness, hiding
Behind their murderous beards and angry wigs.
Still, Gideon says, she looks great in a boiler suit.
Though she never knew what tiredness was until this week
When she pulled double-shift to refit a PT boat.
Tonight she will be too tired to dream of blood-red bandages
Hanging from the walls of the Alexander Palace.
Or of the spoiled little prince in her father's arms.
Or brushing Anastasia's hair a hundred-thousand times
Until it flows like the sparkling Neva on a summer's night.

On Seeing a Digital Map of the Ancient World

The past is a clever bastard, reaching across time
With words that whisper the exotic, giving a Titian glow
To dead countries and cities that imprison us
Within our own imagination and keep it alive.
I never had to ask where Abyssinia was on any map.
In a moment I could be there, on the hills out of Massawa.
The city glistening in the salt-light of the Red Sea, the dust
Of the caravan in my face and hair, a hundred camels
Bringing coffee, ivory and gold to the Highlands.
And what was Abyssinia but the beautiful, burning
Idea of a place, somewhere on the road to Eden; the same
Fantasy that brought the spear carrying Hittites to Anatolia
And the green fingered Kassites to Babylon.

Inishshark

Inishshark is a small island near County Galway The last inhabitants were evacuated in 1960.

On the last day for the island, the last man prepared supper
For his two dead sons, his huge hands calming
The yellow waves of cloth.
On the table he lay Mother's wedding plates, three
Of the four remaining, blue and luminous as the sea
In the mackerel-flickering light.
He had taken two fish from the morning, cooking them gently
In butter and chives, the way the boys liked them.

Later, while waiting in that mistletoe dark, he opened
To the possibility that the island he loved had never loved him.
That in a thousand years of storm and sunshine,
It had never felt the feeble touch of humanity.

Finally, the last man slept.
The clouds hauled in their nets of rain, moonlight
Ran naked on the beach and two young men, happy
And tired from work, dropped the anchor of another day
And went ashore.

Portrait of My Mother as a Surrealist Painting

My mother had her own name.
It was not my father's name.
She was not cunning; she had no need to be.
She was not innocent; she had no need to be.
When she opened the lock of herself it was for love of us.
There was no filter between her feelings
And her thoughts, between her thoughts
And her words, between her words and those she loved.
If Magritte painted her, it would be as a shiny
Electric plug, earthed like Eve, and plunged into
The socket of the World.
And if you brought this painting to her, explaining
That this was her, a portrait by a great painter, she would laugh,
And laugh, until the colours flowed from their appointed places
And splashed on the laughter melting floor.

Study of My Father for a Painting by Rembrandt

Rembrandt would have liked my father.
He had the lived-in face of a Persian King.
Splendidly arrayed in silks and heavenly cloths, his turban
At a slightly jauntier angle than the original,
He would have made a perfect Belshazzar, looking
Suitably uncomfortable—now that the writing
Was on the wall—among Nebuchadnezzar's gold and silver
Stolen from the Holy Temple in Jerusalem.
Afterwards, looking over the great man's shoulder,
He would have made some suggestions on composition.
Perhaps the background could be a fuller, richer black,
A ruby of red beneath the scribed darkness.
He would have brought some memento home with him.
Some fake gold plate or wooden crown, something for us
To play with and feed the wolves of our imagination.

Morning: Rathfarnham

Today, I've made the responsible choice to leave
Yesterday's me in bed and go for a long walk.
Morning is everywhere and soon I'm drenched in it.
I know some of the faces but not all these people
Hurrying by, carrying their closed and secret lives.
Today, I'm a morning person, at one
With the schoolchildren and the businessmen
And that determined woman, perched high in her SUV.
Or this bus driver, whose bus is leaning against the pavement
With the weight of passengers. What is he thinking?
Perhaps, he is still feeling the morning heat of his wife
Or remembering Springtime in Kosovo.
I walk past the minutes rolling downhill towards Rathfarnham.
I resist the temptation to reach out and try to stop them.

Salome

Afterwards, they walked through the palace, her head
On the King's shoulder, his hand encouraging the liquid, easy
Rhythm of her hips.
When, at last, he left her, she watched him navigate
The staggered courtyard and climb the tower
To the bedroom of her insatiable mother.
Her path brought her through the lower parts of the palace.
One candle spluttered in the voiceless kitchen, all the little birds
Of pandemonium locked away.
Her monstrous shadow slid over soft waves of Dead Sea linen
And shrouded baskets of bread and fruit.
It was then she found the platter—bloody and silver heavy.
It seemed to glow there, among the pots and earthen vessels
And the despoiled dishes of the feast.

The House of Mary in Ephesus

Up the steps of the Temple, Morning carries the sleepy Sun.
The house of the stranger is still in darkness.
Mary, already about her stations, stops to listen to John
Crying in his sleep.
As she moves about the house, her movements are deliberate,
As if every moment on Earth is to be savoured.
A man passes on the Jerusalem road.
He is young and handsome and carries lightly
The tool-sack of a carpenter.
Mary watches until he is a small speck on the horizon.
When he is gone, she turns again to her chores.
Now, Morning lifts the Sun over the white roses at the window.
Suddenly, the room where Mary kneels is blazing in light.

My Daughter Has Trouble with Colour

One day my daughter asked me
If everything was in black and white
When we were young.
And I told her it was, as I remember it.
But white then was much whiter and richer
Than today's white, we called it Persil white.
And the women then gleamed under
White parasols, lit by the white sun.
And all the men wore black suits—suits that held
Four different kinds of black, stitched
Into the fibers, so that one could see
The unique and relative luminance
Of Mourning, Luxury, Evil and Darkness.
Now her teacher has rung to tell me
My daughter has trouble with colour.
He doesn't laugh when I say
She is taking after me.

On Seeing Van Gogh's "Starry Night" in New York

We were virgins in New York and the city already
Had us in every possible way.
In the foyer of the Museum of Modern Art, we fell to tears,
As all around us, stars exploded and warm blue
And yellow paint dripped down our startled faces, until
We licked and tasted its genius on our useless tongues.
How many years have I waited for that sensation to come again?
That Venus might step beyond the scoop of her shell
And into her humanity, her feet trailing water across the floor
Of the Uffizi—wrapping her long hair round me, until
I am blind and lost in the pounding heartbeat of the sea.

Kintsugi

Kintsugi, is a Japanese repair technique which uses urushi (Japanese lacquer) dusted with powdered gold to restore broken ceramic and porcelain vessels.

This was the time after, when the house was still
Full of adjusting families, most of them packed
And ready to return to their far-away homes.
Sisters and brothers who had allowed years to fall
Between them, prepared themselves to pull
Away from the obduracy of their mother's death.
In the whispering kitchen, they steadied
Their nerves to say goodbye to their father.
They found the old man in his workshop, surrounded
By lacquer and rice paste, preparing the edges
Of a broken bowl, Ming Dynasty, for repair.
One by one they kissed him goodbye.
His paper-thin skin, almost translucent with age, never
Once bloomed to the heat of emotion.
Weeks later, when the *urushi* had hardened,
He applied the smooth and yellow paste where each
Broken piece grabbed its brother in a deathlike grip.
Now, streams of gold flow through the blue
Ceramic body of a dragon, making the bowl
Whole and beautiful in its perfect imperfection.

Teaching My Daughter to Write Poetry

"Words are not enough to express what I want to say," she said.
And we considered how, when one tries to capture
Joy or pain, or any real feeling, they disappear under
The pressure of wanting, leaving only the frustrated
Ghosts of themselves.
"Perhaps," I said, *"you are an artist at heart, perhaps painting*
Might get you closer to yourself."
"Colour is not enough to express what I want to say," she said.
And we considered how colours affect the brain's pathways
And how every colour has a wavelength, but for her
The lift of each wave has within it its own death.
"It's been lovely Dad," she said, *"but I have to get going."*
At the door I asked her about College and her friends and if
She had managed to get the tickets for that concert, and if
She needed any money and if her bike was still holding up
And what time would she ring me on Friday?
And wasn't it a pity that there was no piano in her apartment.
"Perhaps," I said, *"you are a musician at heart."*
And I started to remind her of the times we used to play
Chopsticks together—but she was already gone.

Shooting Michael Collins

We're waiting all day in *Béal na mBláth* to shoot Michael Collins.
But the sun won't behave for the Director of Photography.
Collins is played by a Northern actor with a tall Cork accent
That ricochets around the damp and darkening vale.
The cameramen are scattered on the hillside, having to move
With the everchanging light to get the best and clearest shot,
While the road twists and turns as if it doesn't know where it's going.
In any case, we only own it for another hour and then we head back
To Bandon for a shower, a meal, and a pint by the fire in Brady's.
There, the man who plays Dev, sits by himself to practice his tears.
From her suite of rooms, the American Superstar rings down.
She wants to try on Kitty Kiernan's wedding dress one more time.

The Women's Sea Bathing Club of Achill Sound

Morning has just stepped through Night's closing gate
And a little cold sun shines inside each raindrop.
Here come the women—they never miss a day—
Eight or nine or ten of them; they cross the strand
At a run, linked together by laughter.
The sea and the women embrace in the foam.
The shock of that first touch—and then the familiar—
The old, salty and familiar.
They swim for a while but their happiness cannot stay submerged.
They begin to sing.
Their voices carry across the new day.
Down the dunes and the drowned fields.
Down the empty streets of the village asleep.
Out in the bay, the men throw down their hauling nets and listen.

The First Time I Saw You I Was Thrown Down
For Cathy on our Wedding Anniversary

The first time I saw you I was thrown down, as the wind
Is thrown when it comes charging from the North
In all its icy armour and sweeps over Errigal and sees
The beauty of the land, and gasps, and dies, falling
Soft as the soft rain falls on the blazing trees of Autumn.
Then my innocence shivered in the streams
And my heart pounded with the sun.
We walked for miles—following the sheep
As they trod their muddy maps of nationhood—until
We reached the mountain's snowy breast.
There we spoke, and there we knew we had found our truth.
And for the first and last time my soul entered another human being.
If we had nothing, we would always have the fleece of that day.
We sometimes take it down and wrap our bodies in it
Until our hair, and hands, and faces, are golden once again.

The Promenade at Bray with a View of the Sugarloaf

Though we were gloved and coated like Eskimos, the wind
Blew us away and pierced our bones until our insides
Were as clean as a child's soul.
You said, *"Let's go down to the shore,"* which
Would have seemed reasonable on any other day.
We traversed the salty pebbles, losing and regaining
Our legs, until, at last, we stood on Bray's thin smile of sand.
Then we played our parts, cartoon characters, laughing
And retreating from the unpredictability of the waves.
Slowly we warmed to the happiness of being together.
So that when the car doors closed with the dead thump
Of endings, we would not let go of the day's sweet intensity.
We took it home as if it was a precious and recovered treasure.

The Postman

Our Postman has a new face—
It's stamped with innocence and all the openness
Of a letter from a grandchild.
"When is the funeral," I ask.
But he knows nothing of Joe, our Old Postman
Or Joe's misfortune, and only has
A red parcel from Denmark to deliver.
I watch him cross the road to Flanigan's,
Every step proclaiming his originality.
At O'Shea's, Vera asks him the same question.
One by one the doors open
And swallow the news, good and bad.
My wife comes in from the garden.
"When is the funeral," she asks.
Before I can reply, she takes the parcel
And heads upstairs—she likes to protect me
From her wilder speculations.
Later, I go to check the internet for news of Joe.
Then I realise, I never knew his second name.

The Face of O'Donovan Rossa

From a coffee-table book of Ireland, the mesmerizing face
Of O'Donovan Rossa looked up at me from history.
His manhood clad in the shabbiest of circumstances—
His criminal name tied round his neck—he stared at me
With the calm intensity of an Apostle on his way to die.
So, this is what it is to believe in a cause, a religion, a man.
It wasn't Yeats's poetry that sent young men and women
Out into the streets to die.
Pearce didn't set himself on fire at the graveside of a poet.
People don't die for poetry.
But no one could look into the blue of those eyes and not know
That this man had eaten bread with the gods.

The Marriage of Strongbow and Aoife at the National Gallery

Before we were married, when I lived alone on the South Circular Road
And you with your parents in Rialto, the National Gallery
Often took us in. There, we learned something about art, but
The way we looked at the paintings told us more about each other
And how we saw the world in those years of innocence.
On our grand tour, we often stood in silence before
Daniel Macalise's painting of the Marriage of Strongbow and Aoife.
Strongbow—the conquering mass of him, his black armour
Scarred with hurts, smoke still swilling about him from the towering
Fires of Waterford—weighs heavy on the stolen land.
Aoife, moves to take her place, her father's hand urgent
At her back, vindication and fear in his eyes.
With a painting larger than my £3-a-week flat, old Daniel
Meant to impress us with the painting's historical contiguity,
Dazzling brushwork and sheer artistry.
But all you saw was a young girl in the grip of circumstances.
And all I saw was men doing what they have always done.
On our honeymoon, we chased desire across Ireland,
The landscape a great painting, with field after field of bones.

Blue Sandwiches
For Pauline Mary Chalifour 1945-2020

Here in Whitehorse, Alaska, in the rain that is almost snow,
We sing the songs of loss and longing.
Repeating your story to each other, jealously
Holding tight to your affection, passing it along, carefully,
Because it is the truth.
We have become the keepers in the story of your life.
We tell it again so you can be once more
Among us, like old times.
You came, young as new day, sunny from Australia.
Leaving the sunburnt arms of your rough-and-ready brothers
And the adoration of your sisters, to embrace
The exhilaration of the North.
You were blown away in Dawson
By a dance and caught by a passing dancer.
You had blue sandwiches at your wedding
To match your dress, because that is who you are.
Together, we carry you through time.
We pull you closer, like the beautiful quilts you made.
It helps to keep us warm against the future.

László Kovács and His Sons Cross the Border

The last Russian soldiers left Hungary in 1991.

The Russian border guards are slow to leave
Their bewildered prisoners. But for a song
They sell their watches, helmets, all the gear
That turns a man into a soldier and a soldier
Back into a man but they take with them
All the forensic evidence of their existence.
Days later, László takes his two blonde sons
Out of their grey school. Outside, he tries
To shake them free but the grey is inclined
To hold on. With some colourful manipulation
Of his hands, he produces two of the whitest
Flowers of Hungary and locates them under
The boy's jumpers, under their shirts, hard
Against the quietness of their boyish hearts.
Then he places them in the small, metal egg
Of his car and drives to the border post
With Austria, where he crosses and crosses
And crosses again, testing their future.

Cleaning Day

Our cleaning-lady is ambivalent on the question
Of Russia's invasion of Ukraine.
She's got her own problems—her father just died
In Moldova, somewhere difficult and beautiful to pronounce.
So, she is full up on the hurting front.
She asks if we remembered to buy Brillo pads this time
And waits to be disappointed.
We assure her that everything is as per her instructions.
She checks the cleaning-box anyway, her movements quick
As a machine-gun turret.
Satisfied, she nods our dismissal, and we leave her to her work.
We drive to the supermarket where stocks are low
And prices are high.
On the way home the News pounds on the thin walls of our
confidence.
"Mariupol evacuation fails for the second time."
In the Carpathian mountains, tanks are shaking the trees
Until every soul-shaped leaf is on the ground.

Song of the Fairy Wren

*While still in the embryonic state, Fairy Wrens sing to their chicks
and this acts as a familial password. A cuckoo sometimes lays its egg
in the wren's nest but only the chicks that have this song are fed.*

Like Fairy Wrens, they had a secret code
That bound them as a family, tight.
Until one day their Mother looked at each
Upturned face as if they belonged to someone else—
So many cuckoos in a fragile nest.
And she took them out into the dark.
Some of them had never seen moonlight.
And the darkness frightened them.
They went for miles in slicks of rain, until,
In the hooded pram, the youngest began to cry.
Soon, over him, his mother's face, beautiful
As a risen moon, made him smile.
Then Mother sat and wept, the children gathering
To comfort her with their song.

At the Arkadiko Bridge

Arkadiko Bridge is a 3000-year-old chariot bridge in Greece.

Phaëton was setting the Earth on fire as we parked
Our hired car and walked the Tityn road to the bridge, humped
As it was over the dead river of a long dead people.
We sat on the hillside and looked back across time.
Then came the soundless chariots, carrying
The spear-laden soldiers of someone's dream, the men
Of Pylos, Midea, Thebes, Athens and Thessaly.
From noon to sunset we watched them cross, fantastic
In their boar-tusk helmets, shields and armour, horseshit everywhere.
And as the sun set, their gangling reins, studded
With ivory and metal, threw up a jewel-like glittering
Until the hillside was butterflied with light, light that lit our faces,
As if we were real and everything was not a dream.

The Tree of Life

In 1962, Cambridge University's Francis Crick, James Watson and Maurice Wilkins received the Nobel Prize for the discovery of the double helix structure in DNA. Their colleague, Rosalind Franklin, whose famous X-ray, Photo 51, had shown the first helix, died four years earlier.

She ate her lunch beneath King's old chestnut tree,
Its Ent like arms more extreme than J.R.R Tolkien's
Walking and talking imagination.
The leafy shade, with its flashes of sunlight,
Allowed the X-rays to darken and flare
In her hands and gave a quality of God whispering.
Sometimes she saw nothing before her.
Yet, when discovery seemed close, she gloried
In the times and in her undoubted destiny.
And, when she heard the bells of Great St Mary's
Welcome a Christening or a Wedding, she would lean
Contented against the twisted trunk, as the chimes
Rose above all, telling life's real story.

The House in Rialto

Your old house in Rialto once had an upright piano
Where silver framed photographs jostled for attention.
Though we barely knew each other then,
I once had a place there, sitting with your family, smiling
As if I was all grown up and twenty-one, although
I was only nineteen—the youngest nineteen that ever lived.
Thank God I was so young.
Had I been any older, I would have known
That the whole thing was impossible.

Today, in Rialto, there is only me, standing in the empty house,
Watching a family of foxes stretch their legs in the sunshine.
But I have work to do.
I must clear the yard of weeds and briars and keep
The whole place looking respectable—
For memory's sake.
Later, at the door of our home, I listen and wait until
You are finished playing *Clair de Lune* on the old upright piano.

Learning to Play Pétanque in Tuileries Garden
For Eleanor and Brendan

The crowd surrounds the Louvre like fans
At a rock concert, but we are away—away
In the tree-quiet, heart-quiet corner of Tuileries,
Where Paris stops selling itself to everyone
And asks if it can be yours—yours alone.
Two young Parisians from Ireland are teaching us to play
Pétanque, each metal ball landing in a soft crunch
And rolling across the sacred ground of France—
Silver apples tumbling from Yeats's pocket.
Before my throw, I stand in the gold-dappled light, taking
Everything this day has to give, enumerating
Reasons to believe in the everlastingness of all things.

Egyptian Blue

In the corridors of Yale they search the ancient rubble
Of Mesopotamia for Egyptian Blue, the lost colour of Ashurbanipal,
The last great king of Assyria.
The royal colour once adorned the flying jinn's of Nineveh
And the palace library of Kalhu, where the story of the Flood
Was baked into tablets of clay by the conquering fires of Babylon.
A flake of paint is gathered from the thigh of a eunuch
And held under the unflinching eye of a microscope.
His bow and arrows the colour of Dragon's Blood, his mace
And beard and broken pieces held together by memory and resin.
From ninety-three-million-miles away, light bathes
The Tree of Life in glassy, arsenic yellow.
In the basement, the Tigris has burst its banks, sweeping
Professors and scholars onto rocks of lapis lazuli.

The Yellow Wagtail

While waiting for the Pharmacy to dispense
Its temporary absolution, I rounded the local park.
Here, where the maps show a river, the fat Dodder
Struggled to fit its winter coat.
Suddenly, the day deposited a small brightness
On the opposite bank.
A wagtail, yellowed in flash, alive in the ceaseless balance
Of its body, bobbing in and out of reality.
I don't know much about birds but I had never seen a wagtail
Carrying its own sunshine.
As it flounced its rarity across the day, I found myself
Watching it with the kind of wonderment
Of the first man for the first bird.
It seemed to want to show me every detail of itself, down
To the soft, brown necklace of feathers on its throat.
Later, I learned that it was the bird of the god Atum,
Who created himself by saying his own name.

The Burning of the Books

She left her religion in our care.
Her old prayerbooks and Bible, lapped by mould
And intoxicated by time.
Immediately, we felt the flutter of her anxiety.
We all agreed, the books were too far gone.
Their words tumbling to the floor, detached
From their sacredness.
As we piled them high in the hearth,
I was vaguely aware of something wrong, remembering,
I suppose, old tales of hate against all books,
When even thoughts were set on fire.
It was many days before I put a match to them.
And even then I wasn't sure.
As the blaze took hold of the Bible, something small
And worm-like-wriggled from between the pages of Genesis
And the illiterate flames roared with unthinking joy
As they burned the beautiful, perfumed trees of Eden.

Tiger
For my Grandchildren

You are now entering a dangerous poem, please keep
Your hands inside the lines at all times.
This is a Tiger poem.
There is no certainty as to the number of tigers in this poem.
It could be one or two—not counting the one right behind you –
Or a thousand or even as many tigers as there are on the planet –
Imagine that.
Imagine five thousand tigers.
That's a lot for a poem but not a lot for a whole planet.
Imagine them prowling between these lines – their grace,
And latent, casual power.
How exotic.
How wonderful.
This one won't bite.
So, it's ok to bring your hand close, closer—HOLD IT!
Not that close.
No need to take chances, after all, even if this is only a poem,
It is a wild poem, and he is a wild creature.
He seems more real now, when you can see the stripes
Up close and the skin ripple along his back.
Now, as the whiskers touch the inside of your hand
You smell the guts of sambar deer on his breath.
I see your eyes are glued to his teeth.
I don't blame you.
But, no need to be nervous.
He seems disinterested … for the moment.

First Chair

How wonderful it is when your mother is first chair
In the Orchestra and the music that trills
Her body, brightens round you in the womb.
And outside of the heaven that is only you and her,
Rivers of music are flowing outwards, drenching
The people and taking them to a place of joy.
Tonight, both your hearts are pounding much too fast.
Then the first notes fall into you and you melt into
A contentment that is almost a state of grace.
Tonight, another great composer shows the world,
With Violins, Violas, Cellos, Drums, French-horns,
Bassoons and the chocolate-notes of the Clarinet,
What it feels like to be touched by Eternal Love.

The Louis Copeland Suit

He was a twelve-year-old Caravaggio boy, without
The knowing smile, a patch shaped like Australia
On his corduroy trousers, that first day at Secondary School.
And in his hand he held a sweaty promissory note.
A promise by his out-of-work father, written hastily
The night before, that school fees would be paid.
Now in *Louis Copeland's,* the Manager asks him to feel
The richness of the fabric, rolling between his experienced
Thumb and forefinger the woolen cloth that fills him
With a kind of awe, as if he touched the robes of a Saint.
This is a bespoke suit, the Manager tells him, with fused
Lining and stitching of such precision, any heart-surgeon
In Ireland would be proud to claim it as his work.
See how the whole thing comes together, the fit, the drape,
The buttonholes, and the rather special boutonniere loop.
The material, carefully chosen by someone, is classic grey,
With barely perceptible veins of red running through it.
He tells anyone who will listen—he doesn't usually spend
This kind of money on a suit—it's for his daughter's wedding.
The Manager asks if she lives here, in Ireland.
No, he tells him—she's coming home—from Australia.

Dreamtime Sequence in Ballarat

At night, in Australia, by a small lake, tired, jet-lagged
Understanding only the sacredness of the grandchild
In my arms—the tour guide switches on the darkness.
The first sound of the new world is the flap of giant wings.
Bundjil, the Creator, the eagle, rises out of nothing
And from nothing becomes light.
Also made of light are his wives and his son, Bibbeal the Rainbow
And his brother, Pailian the bat.
Now they sing the Song of Creation.
It is like no song I have ever heard and yet I know every note.
It is lifting me out of myself, all my colours falling.
I am my Past, Present and Future self, flowing towards Eternity.
And then it is over.
And we return to the comfort and humanity of the bus.
Homeward, we cross the little mountains of Ballarat, the children
Kissed by sleep, the adults disturbed, soulful shamans.
I put my arms around my family and hold them close.

Evensong

A few things have come together
And for the first time in a while
I'm feeling like myself, driving
To Michael Farry's book launch in Trim.
It's the furrowed and uneven month of March
And it's after six, but the day is unwilling
To let the light go home.
The clouds are dark, they could be nothing else
But their skirts are a gold, pinkish colour
The way my brother Greg paints them
In his visions of the heart rocking Burren in Clare.
Here and there in the greening landscape,
There is the glow of fires without fire.
Almost there now and the roads are getting smaller.
Near Scurlogstown, two huge oak trees settle crows
Into their black cups.
All of a sudden I feel uneasy—in these terrible times
It must be wrong to love the world so much.

Eternal Return

"What if some day or night a demon were to steal after you into your loneliest loneliness, and say to you, "This life as you now live it and have lived it, you will have to live once more and innumerable times more." ~Friedrich Nietzsche

There was a time—a time when I was very young—
When I believed that I would grow into my future, old
And sage and full of poetry and leave the hurtful things
Of the world to those who can only live by wounding.
And, by God's kindness, sufficiently happy I would end.
Then, one night, reading by the fire—not in loneliness,
I had locked the doors of all those cages—but open
And half accepting life as it was, Nietzsche appeared,
Dark as a demon in a dream, and we walked together
Until we came to the great rock of his thought.
And there by Lake Silvaplana, in the snows of Sils Maria,
He cried for the joy of eternal pain and eternal happiness.
And when I woke, I found his monster tears upon my cheek.

The Chariot of Selene

One lonely night, deep in January, the Moon
Sat in the back seat of my car, waiting for a ride.
She was perfect, her face expectant and radiant.
I thought about all the places I could take her, all the places
That you and I knew.
In the end, we drove just a few miles.
And at that spot, you know the one I mean,
I took the Moon into the woods and showed her
Where we had first made love.
And there she lay down.
And I lay beside her, among the half-hearted islands of snow.
We lay there for the longest time, looking up at the stars.
And after a while I slept.
And it began to rain.
And the rain shot through the Moon.
And I woke in a pool of moonlight.

The Trade

These old tools have been kissed by the red lips of rust.
These chisels, half their original size – shortened and ground, ground
And honed by my Grandfather, while he chased perfection
Down that never-ending road.
When I think of him, I see him working the sharp edges.
Working with all the intensity of a zealot, a thrilling of sparks
Lighting up the life of that kind old man.
One day I had the nerve to tell him I had fallen in love with poetry
And that I might be a poet.
He stopped the saw in the middle of its satisfying rhythm
And looked at me, as if seeing me for the first time.
He pointed to the dovetailed frame on the bench –
Joints happy in each other, solid and locked in precision.
"There's poetry for you," he said.
And so, I have taken up poetry's claw hammer, its handsaw, its oil
And grindstone, its block plane and its iron vice.
Sometimes you will find me working on the edges, with all the love
And intensity of a zealot, a thrilling of words lighting my room.

The 23rd Sunday in Ordinary Time

At the river, on his way to serve at Mass, he found
Tommy Kelly's cross of flowers knocked sideways
By the rain. He attempted a prayer, but was distracted
By the maggots drowning in the flooded cups.
In the rosewood-dark, he put on his vestments.
Deep inside the Church, the early Christians
Took their places near the radiators to dry their clothes—
Umbrellas discarded like swords under the pews.
At noon, he followed Father Henry out to the clearing
Of throats and the kafuffle that has lived in crowds
Since the beginning of time. Somehow, he missed
His cue to ring the handbells for the Consecration.
Suddenly he rang them, rang and rang them.
Rang them as hard as he could. Louder and louder
They rang, over the headless congregation, out
The Church doors, alarming the Sunday streets.
On and on until they reached the river's edge.

This is What Happened the Day After

Your friends were blue, the colour that often
Denotes sadness, but then they got on with it.
People called you a saint but your saintliness could not be
Attached to anything you did.
People said if you had married you would have made
A great family man and that it would have been nice
If there had been children.
No children were present on the day.
Your modest wealth was calculated to within a few cents.
The elegance of your single debt was remarked upon.
Your sister, who never cries, cried.
Your cousins from Baltinglass stayed in your house.
Your dog ran away.
Your cat came home.
The day was very ordinary, except
That there was no more time to be with you, all
Our next moments were gone, no fireworks or
Affinity or quietness, no whiskey or cigars and all the greys
Meant as much, or as little, as the brightest reds.
Indifference was all.
And the expected flowers arrived too late from Montreal.

Honeymoon

In 1854, Charlotte Bronte married Irishman Arthur Bell Nicholls, her father's curate, and they honeymooned in Ireland. They spent some time in the seaside village of Kilkee, in Co Clare. She became pregnant almost immediately and she died with her unborn child in 1855.

Yesterday, on my walk to the cliffs, I saw Mrs Nicholls
Scribbling away in her notebook as usual.
She wore a Barège dress in the French style, a fantastic design
The colour of green-moss in sunlight.
At times she can look tired, though she is still this side
Of forty, but she is pretty and petite—in the English way.
Across the thistle-clouded fields, her husband came
And they walked together to the edge of the ocean.
She is tiny and barely reaches his elbow.
All the more wonder then, as they surveyed the Atlantic playing
With the little fishing boats, their happiness sang out.
I saw them again today as they left for home, the coach tumbling
With baggage, the Innkeeper fussing, Mrs Nicholls
Smiling to herself as if she carried a delightful secret.

A Thousand Summers
For Ken Rennison

Yesterday, while listening to my granddaughter playing
Chopin, a voice on the phone called to—by-the-way—
Tell me you were gone.
But with your death, you were suddenly alive.
Alive in the places where we grew to boys and men,
Loving, and jealous of each other, reaching out beyond
Ourselves towards something better but unnamed.
Then, only by playing every sweaty game to exhaustion,
Could we quiet the devil who wanted us to bite down
On the juicy, innocent world.
Made safe by time, our escapades make me smile.
Is it too late to thank you for those summers, when
We swam like dolphins in the sea of each other?
Forgive me for using these memories to ease the blow
Of your passing, lately it feels like one blow too many.
In the next room, my granddaughter is playing Chopin.
Each exquisite note living and dying in the same moment

Wearing My Heart on My Sleeve

Because I wear my heart on my sleeve, I caught it
On the needy thorns, whose limbs strain for any kind
Of touch, whose lipstick berries hang
Heavy and red with desire.

Once I lost my heart by the sea, where foaming
Moonlight rises beneath the diamond shingle.
Later I found it among the savage rocks, a mermaid
Rubbing salt into my wounds.

Deep in the green rosary of the mountains, crazed
With grief, I threw my heart away.
I relented, but searching the desolate hills, found
So many hearts, I could hardly tell my own.

The Woman Who Sold Time

Elizabeth Ruth Naomi Belville (5 March 1854 – 7 December 1943), sold Greenwich Mean Time to her clients all over London from the 1794 John Arnold pocket chronometer once owned by her father.

For a few pence you could know exactly where you were
On your journey to Eternity.
And every clock that hung from work-day walls, glowed
With correctness when she touched it.
Then the workers could breathe more easily, immersed
In exactitude. No more Victorian limbo—where Time
Rolled about, lost and careless and without order.
The great clock at Greenwich was synchronised with Heaven
And from its hands she took it—to sell Time in the streets
And the Commonwealth of Offices.
Her father, the Timekeeper, had given her the City
To watch over and pull the uncertain day back from the brink.
Everywhere she went she was a reassurance
That all was right with England.
Sometimes she kept Time and sometimes Time kept her.
Then, after eighty-nine years of courting, they ran way together.

Ron Carey was born in Limerick and now lives in Dublin, Ireland. He has been a prize winner and finalist in many international poetry competitions including, *The Bridport Prize, Lightship International Poetry Prize, Cinnamon Press Poetry Awards, Fish International Poetry Prize, Gregory O' Donoghue International Poetry Awards, Strokestown Poetry Prize, Hugh O'Flaherty Poetry Award, iYeats Poetry Prize, the Wasafiri New Writing Prize for Poetry and the Allingham Poetry Prize.* His poems have appeared in New Irish Writings, the Irish Times as well as many anthologies and magazines. His debut collection, *Distance,* was shortlisted for the Forward Prize Best First Collection UK and Ireland. He runs courses in Creative Writing both online and in person. *A Storm in Arcadia,* is his fourth collection of poetry. www.roncareypoetry.com

www.ingramcontent.com/pod-product-compliance
Lightning Source LLC
Chambersburg PA
CBHW020340130626
46549CB00003B/1229